I SEE THE PROMISED LAND

A LIFE OF MARTIN LUTHER KING JR.

I would like to thank my mother, who passed
on her love for the word, and Gita, Manu and
Tara Books for the gig, I'm honored to be part
of the moment, my mother would be proud
of this one.

   Arthur Flowers

I SEE THE PROMISED LAND

A LIFE OF MARTIN LUTHER KING JR.

ARTHUR FLOWERS
MANU CHITRAKAR
GUGLIELMO ROSSI

Groundwood Books
House of Anansi Press
Toronto   Berkeley

LORD LEGBA, OPEN THIS GATE.

It is I, Rickydoc Trickmaster, ask that this gate be opened, this work be done. I am a Hoodoo Lord of the Delta and power is what I do.

I AM MYTHMAKER.

SIT DOWN WHY DON'T YOU. REST A SPELL. I, MY FRIEND, HAVE A STORY TO TELL.

I suspect you've heard the Martin Luther King story as commonly told, but this a telling replete with the Will of the Gods, with Fate and Destiny and The Human Condition –

WHAT WOULD A TALE BE WORTH WITHOUT THESE THINGS.

IT IS FITTING THAT THIS TALE STARTS

WITH THE BIRTH OF MARTIN LUTHER KING.

UNFORTUNATELY FOR MY PURPOSES THERE IS NOTHING PARTICULARLY MIRACULOUS ABOUT HIS BIRTH, NO CLAIM OF DIVINE PATRIMONY, NO INTERESTING METEOROLOGICAL PHENOMENA.

IT IS HOWEVER PERHAPS SIG-NIFICANT THAT HE IS THE SON,

GRANDSON AND

GREAT GRANDSON

OF SOUTHERN BLACK BAPTIST PREACHERS. THIS, IN FACT, CANNOT BE OVEREMPHASIZED.

1

He has an independent base. The black church one of the few forces in the black community not totally dependent on white patronage. Black preachers have always stood on the front lines of struggle and when it came time to move the people, King just turned his sermonizing skills into political oration.

RUN THOSE BIBLICAL CADENCES, THOSE PROMISELAND RIFFS, YOU HALFWAY THERE WITH BLACKFOLK. THEY WILL WORK W/ YOU.

2

King what they call a raceman, from the progressive wing of the Southern black bourgeoisie, folk for whom racial custodianship is a family tradition.

3

With a Doctorate in Systematic Theology,

KING SAW THE STRUGGLE AS AN INSTRUMENT OF MORAL IMPROVEMENT.

He had been influenced by Thoreau's Civil Disobedience and the example of Mahatma Gandhi to speculate a plan of nonviolent protest and activism. As a budding young theologian King expressed frustration with ministry that concern itself only with well-being in the hereafter. King felt the well-apportioned ministry should also concern itself with well-being in the world.

THE CASE CAN BE MADE THAT MARTIN LUTHER KING WAS BORN TO THE ROLE.

IT IS HIS FA.

NOW THAT DAHOMEY
—FATE, FREE WILL, AI
QUITE SURE HOW THA
CLAIM WITH ALL MY
MARTIN LUTHER KIN
TEMPLE THAT NIGHT
PROMISELAND. IT WA
THE BALCONY OF TH
THAT NEXT MORNIN
FATED TO BE THE AN
IS TO US NOW. IT IS H

FA A FUNNY THING

THAT – I'M NOT

WORK BUT I DO

OWER THAT IT WAS

'S FA TO BE IN THE

HE SAY HE SEEN THE

HIS FA TO BE ON

LORRAINE MOTEL

I CLAIM HE WAS

ESTRAL CALL HE

FA.

NOW FA DON'T JUST DROP INTO YOUR LAP.

IT REQUIRE YOUR UNDIVIDED ATTENTION.

In his heart young King aspired to an academic position, a life of study and meditation, but he decided, emulating his own professors, that a pastorate would be an appropriate 1st step. How will you, young King, master Systematic Theology, if you have not been baptized in the field so to speak. So he take up the pastorate of the Dexter Baptist Church in Montgomery, Alabama.

IN DOING SO HE STEP FORTHRIGHTLY ONTO THE HOODOO BOARD OF DESTINY.

Now, just 'cause you got the power doesn't necessarily mean you will be touched by the hard hand of destiny.

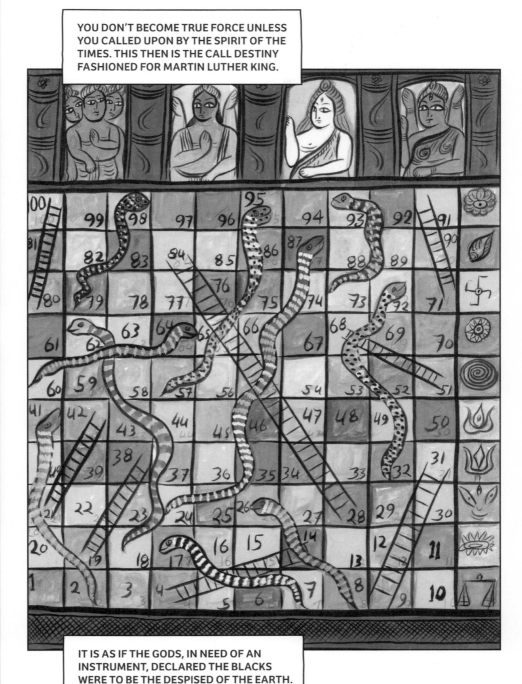

YOU DON'T BECOME TRUE FORCE UNLESS YOU CALLED UPON BY THE SPIRIT OF THE TIMES. THIS THEN IS THE CALL DESTINY FASHIONED FOR MARTIN LUTHER KING.

IT IS AS IF THE GODS, IN NEED OF AN INSTRUMENT, DECLARED THE BLACKS WERE TO BE THE DESPISED OF THE EARTH.

THE BLACKS
ARE DECIMATED.

IT IS THE BLACKS OF WEST AFRICA THAT CONCERN US HERE,

CAPTURED,

ENSLAVED,

MANACLED AND MARCHED TO THE COAST,

WAREHOUSED IN THE COASTAL CASTLES OF SHAME, GHANA'S CAPE COAST,

SENEGAL'S GOREE ISLAND,

THESE MUST BE EXPERIENCED TO BE BELIEVED, TO BE UNDER-STOOD, OUR ANCESTORS WAREHOUSED LIKE PRODUCE UNTIL THEY ARE STACKED ONTO SLAVESHIPS PACKFAT W/ HUMAN CARGO,

men, women and children basting in their own waste, sunk in despair and confusion –

WHAT IS THIS PLACE,

WHO ARE THESE PEOPLE,

WHAT HAS BECOME OF US (THE MIDDLE PASSAGE THAT'S WHAT) –

HOW MANY MILLION DEAD,

TOSSED OVERBOARD TO FEED WILY SHARKS THAT FOLLOW EACH SHIP,

HOW MANY LEAP OF THEIR OWN ACCORD.

Atlantic
Ocean

CARIBBEAN

Dominican
Republic

San Juan

Antigua
and
Barbuda

St. Kitts
and Nevis

Dominica

St. Vincent
and the
Grenadines

St. Lucia

Grenada

Barbados

Trinidad
and
Tobago

Caracas

Venezuela

Atlantic
Ocean

AMERICA

ince

THE SLAVE BUILT COLONIES OF KINGSTON,

SÃO PAULO,

PORT-AU-PRINCE,

HAVANA,

BOSTON,

CHARLESTON

AND THE GEORGIA SEA ISLANDS,

THESE CAPITAL LINKS IN THE UNHOLY CHAINS OF SLAVERY.

This is the testing. For the Gods' purposes they must be stripped to the essence and what better scourge of souls than slavery.

BLACKS ARE TREATED LIKE SOME INHUMAN LIVESTOCK. WORKED TO DEATH. USED AS SEXUAL PLAYTHINGS.

THEY ARE AT THE TOTAL DISCRETION OF THEIR MASTERS. IT IS LIFE AND DEATH ON A WHIM.

THE BLACKS RESIST, BOTH
ACTIVELY AND PASSIVELY

Some become runaways.

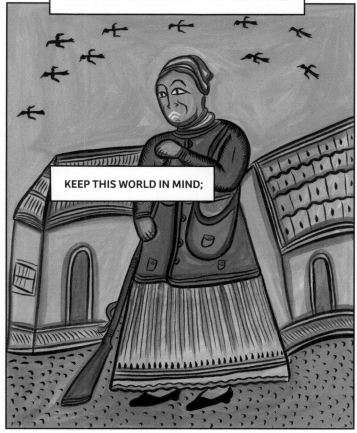

THIS IS THE WORLD MARTIN LUTHER KING WAS BORN INTO.

The apartheid South of Martin Luther King's day was little changed from the days of slavery.

TRUE,

slavery had been outlawed during the Civil War by the Emancipation Proclamation of 1863,

BUT THE KU KLUX KLAN, RECONSTRUCTION AND THE BLACK LAWS IMMEDIATELY PUSH BLACKFOLK BACK INTO THE QUASI SLAVERY OF SHARECROPPING.

SHARECROPPING A FEUDAL SYSTEM.

OLDSCHOOL. YOU WORK THE LAND AND YOU PAY OUT A PART OF YOUR CROP.

But by the time settling up come round you owe the man so much for this and that you never get out from under and you totally submissive,

YESSIR NOSIR
ALL THE TIME,

ROUND THE TURN OF THE 20TH CENTURY, A GREAT MULTITUDE OF BLACKFOLK LEFT THE SOUTH IN WHAT'S BEEN CALLED

THE GREAT MIGRATION—

a mass movement that turn a troubled rural folk into an

EQUALLY TROUBLED URBAN FOLK.

So, now you got two contingents of blackfolk,

NORTH AND SOUTH.

NORTH, THE RACISM MORE SUBTLE, DISCRIMI-NATION MORE GRACEFUL,

BUT IN THE SOUTH IT IS STRAIGHT OUT OPPRESSION. BUCK NAKED APARTHEID.

Hard to explain to people what life was like in the apartheid South. Perhaps if you are an Untouchable of India, a black in the Sudan,

PERHAPS THEN YOU KNOW.

YOU EXPECTED AT ALL TIMES TO DEFER TO WHITE-FOLK, TO SIT IN THE BACK OF THE BUS, TO DRINK FROM THE COLORED WATER FOUNTAIN, TO STEP OFF THE SIDEWALK IF WHITEFOLK COMING AT YOU.

BLACKFOLK TREATED LIKE THEY NOT QUITE HUMAN.

CLOSE BUT NOT QUITE.

41

BLACKS WHO DO CHALLENGE THE STATUS QUO

are often deprived of livelihood, homes and sometime their lives.

NIGHT RIDERS AND LYNCHINGS VERY PREVALENT IN THOSE TRANSITIONAL YEARS.

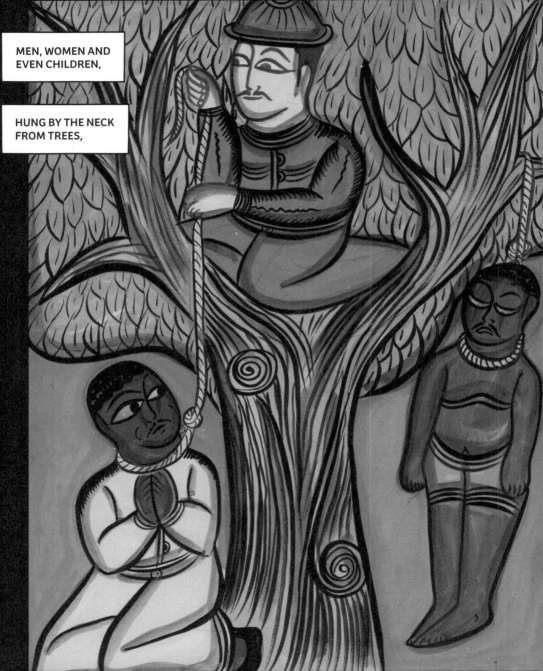

MEN, WOMEN AND
EVEN CHILDREN,

HUNG BY THE NECK
FROM TREES,

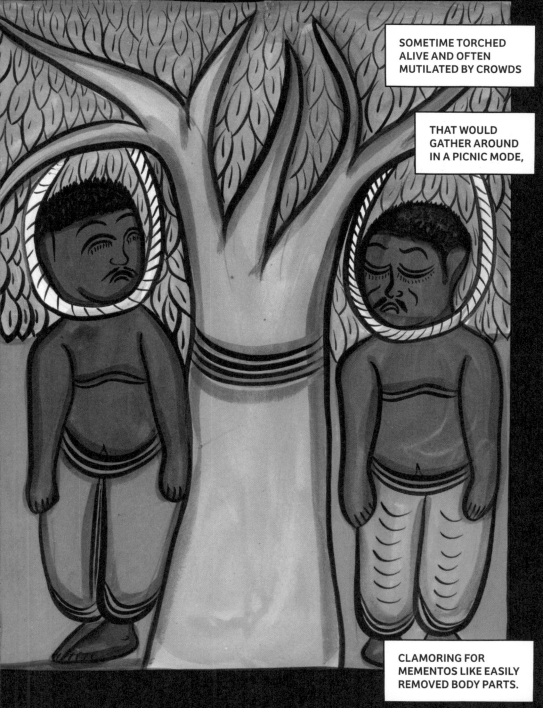

This is the world into which Martin Luther King is born.

THIS THE WORLD THAT PROVIDE

THE CALL HE COME TO ANSWER.

Young Martin is expected, of course, to follow in the august footsteps of his father, his grandfather and his great grandfather as pastor of Ebenezer Baptist,

THE MONTGOMERY BUS BOYCOTT 1955:

The Touch of Destiny's Hand.

NOW, I SUSPECT YOU KNOW THE STORY, AT LEAST WHAT EVERYBODY ELSE KNOW.

MONTGOMERY, ALABAMA, 1955,

THE RULE IS BLACKFOLK HAVE TO SIT IN THE BACK OF THE BUS, CAN'T SIT IN THE WHITE SECTION, HAVE TO STAND IN THE BLACK SECTION IF A WHITE PERSON WANT TO SIT.

But on this particular day, Sister Rosa Parks' feet are tired and she don't feel like standing. So, she sat there on the hard rock of destiny and found it to her liking.

Local leader E.D. Nixon had been looking for a case he could use to challenge the bus laws and institute a direct action campaign. He recognize Sister Parks for the Blessing she is, somebody the community would defend and support. So. He call together the activist leaders of black Montgomery. They form the Montgomery Improvement Association, and

THE LEGENDARY MONTGOMERY BUS BOYCOTT IS ON.

NOW MARTIN LUTHER NEW TO MONTGOMERY. TOOK UP THE DEXTER CHURCH POST IN A BID TO ESCAPE THE LONG SHADOW OF DADDY KING AND HAD THROWN HIMSELF INTO MINISTERING HIS PASTORATE. THIS WHERE HE FORM HIS LIFELONG PARTNERSHIP WITH RALPH ABERNATHY. THEY BOTH MEMBERS OF THE ACTIVIST WING OF MONTGOMERY'S MINISTRY.

BUT HE ONLY BEEN THERE ABOUT A YEAR OR SO, SO WHEN TIME COME TO NOMINATE THE LEADERSHIP OF THE MONTGOMERY IMPROVEMENT ASSOCIATION,

KING IS NOMINATED MOSTLY BECAUSE HE IS NOT ONE OF THE ENTRENCHED FACTIONS.

HE TAKE ON LEADERSHIP RELUCTANTLY.

HE FELT UNPREPARED, BUT WHO IS PREPARED WHEN FA CALL.

IT IS IN THE DOING THAT YOU GAIN THE GRACE.

The factions thought they had in King a malleable instrument that would take the heat if it all fell apart. It wasn't until he spoke at the 1ˢᵗ mass meeting with the community that the factions realize they had stumbled into the lap of destiny.

MLK A MACK. A MASTER OF THE WORD.

AN ORATOR OF HISTORICAL POWER, STATURE AND SIGNIFICANCE.

A MAN WITH A VISION.

"IF WE PROTEST COU
YET WITH DIGNITY A
WHEN THE HISTORY
IN THE FUTURE, SOM
TO SAY, 'THERE LIVE
OF BLACK PEOPLE, O
THE MORAL COURAG
FOR THEIR RIGHTS. A
INJECTED A NEW MEA
VEINS OF HISTORY A

RAGEOUSLY, AND
D CHRISTIAN LOVE,
OOKS ARE WRITTEN
BODY WILL HAVE
A RACE OF PEOPLE,
PEOPLE WHO HAD
TO STAND UP
D THEREBY THEY
NING INTO THE
D CIVILIZATION.'"

Some folk that was there that 1st
evening call it The Great Awakening.

He had not yet solidified his non-violence strategies. As all good things tend to do, that came out in the crucible of struggle, but you can see the seeds in his view of the Movement as a moral struggle and his evolving vision of the African American's role in America's destiny. And the destiny of the world too.

BOY GOT THAT LONGGAME VISION PUT EVERYTHING IN A STRATEGIC CONTEXT.

This is a good thing. For I would you my people be masters of strategy, the key that opens all locks. But I digress.

A GOOD STORY YOU GOT TO KEEP THE PIECES IN ORDER. ILLUMINATION IS A PROCESS AND THE LAYERS OF UNDERSTANDING MUST BE PRECISELY LAID.

They set up carpools that defy tickets and all manner of harassment; both the hale and the canefolk walk the walk and defy all attempts to intimidate them.

The powers that be cooperate by refusing all redress.

IT IS THE LAW, THEY INSIST.

WE CAN'T GO AGAINST THE LAW, PEOPLE.

THEN WHERE WOULD WE BE.

THAT FIRST DAY KING AND THE MIA LEADERSHIP DON'T KNOW WHAT TO EXPECT.

BUT WHEN BUS AFTER BUS GO BY EMPTY THEY KNEW THEN THAT BLACKFOLK HAD DECIDED TO STRUGGLE.

THIS IN ITSELF IS NEW.

The thing that most distress young King about Southern apartheid is black acquiescence in their own oppression.

TOO MANY OF THEM ACCEPT INFERIORITY AS THEIR GIVEN PLACE.

BUT FOR 385 DAYS,

the blacks of Montgomery defy harassment, intimidation, bombs, and all manner of repression.

What was at first a joke to the powers that be became on some parts grudging respect, on some parts unreasoning anger.

Montgomery's intransigence convince the blacks, as Frederick Douglass once noted,

POWER CONCEDES NOTHING WITHOUT DEMAND.

They will have to make Montgomery give it up.

HOW DARE THEY CHALLENGE US. HOW DARE THEY CHALLENGE OUR WAY OF LIFE.

SO BLACKFOLK COMMENCE TO WALKING,

CARPOOLING,

BOOKING,

WHATEVER IT TAKE.

KING IS DELIGHTED. HE ASK ONE OLD WOMAN WALKING BY IF SHE WASN'T TOO OLD FOR THIS, ASK HER IF HER FEET NOT TIRED.

MY FEET IS TIRED SHE SAY, BUT MY SOUL IS RESTED.

HE LIKE THAT.

HE LIKE THAT A LOT.

MADE HIS HEART FULL TO BURSTING.

MONTGOMERY GOT HOT ON HIM

PULICIS

ARRESTS,

DEATH THREATS,

BOMBINGS.

These threats reflect unsettling developments in American culture.

Brown vs. Board of Education had riled up oldschool whitefolk. Next thing they know they got blackfolk sitting in and marching and picketing and freedom riding and all manner of foolishness.

WE DON'T GO TO SCHOOL WITH NEGROES

WE DON'T GO TO SCHOOL WITH NEGROES

WE DON'T GO TO SCHOOL WITH NEGROES

THE OLD SOUTH RESPOND BY CLOSING SCHOOLS AND SWIMMING POOLS,

AND WITH A REVIVAL OF THE KU KLUX KLAN, WHITE CITIZEN COUNCILS,

AND THE VIGILANTE VIOLENCE THAT HAD ALWAYS SERVED THEM SO WELL.

That little Emmett Till fellow, they say he whistled at a whitegirl, they necktied that boy w/barbed wire tied to a cotton gin and

THROWED HIM INTO THE TALLAHATCHIE RIVER.

When King's house got bombed, friends and family back in Atlanta try to talk him out of it.

HE SAY I APPRECIATE YOUR CONCERN

BUT IT'S JUST TOO LATE.

At the mass meetings he kept the good colored folk of Montgomery fired up.

Note that move now; that redeem the soul of America bit. That little bit of ideological orchestration.

THIS WHAT MAKE MARTIN LUTHER KING SPECIAL.

HE SAYING THIS NOT JUST ABOUT US.

THIS ABOUT SAVING EVERYBODY.

KEEP AN EYE ON THIS, NOW.

EQUATING THE BLACK STRUGGLE WITH
THE STRUGGLE FOR HUMAN DIGNITY.

THIS IS WHERE
HE FIND HIS FA.

AFTER 385 DAYS OF STRUGGLE THE SUPREME COURT RULED SEGREGATION IN MONTGOMERY ILLEGAL AND TO THE RELIEF OF THE BUSINESS COMMUNITY THE BUSES DESEGREGATED. THE BLACKS COME BACK,

SITTING WHERE THEY PLEASE.

SCLC AND THE GREAT BLACK BOOK OF GENERATIONS

It is the Montgomery Bus Boycott that add Martin Luther King's name to the Great Black Book of Generations.

IT IS THE MONTGOMERY CAMPAIGN ESTABLISH HIM AS A LEADER, ESTABLISH HIS NONVIOLENCE STRATEGY AS ONE COLORED FOLK EMULATE ALL OVER THE SOUTH.

FOR THESE ARE TUMULTUOUS TIMES AND JUST RIGHT FOR HIS BRAND OF NONVIOLENT CIVIL DISOBEDIENCE.

BLACKS ALL OVER THE SOUTH STAND-
ING UPRIGHT. RAISING UP HEADS BENT
SO LONG THEY MOST FORGOT HOW.

THE JUBILANT VICTORS DECIDE THEY
NEED A MORE FORMAL ORGANIZATION.
ONE BASED ON THE BLACK CHURCH.

**They form the Southern
Christian Leadership Conference
and set up office in Atlanta
with one employee, the
indomitable Ella Baker. Oldline
groups like the NAACP and
the Urban League are wary
of the newcomer.**

MARTIN ASSURES THEM THERE IS
MORE THAN ENOUGH STRUGGLE TO GO
AROUND. HE WOULD STEP ON NO TOES.

Basically this period of King's ministry consist of getting called into struggles to desegregate various cities across the South by local activists in need of King's high profile and strategic resources. Like some Black Belt Pilgrimage, these cities have been entered into the Great Black Book of Generations:

ATLANTA.

MONTGOMERY.

BIRMINGHAM.

LITTLE ROCK.

ST. AUGUSTINE.

SELMA.

WASHINGTON.

CHICAGO.

AND OF COURSE MEMPHIS.

IN HIS BOOK WHERE DO WE GO FROM HERE,

KING CLAIM IT IS A PRIVILEGE TO BECOME INSTRUMENT OF A GREAT IDEA.

He quote Toynbee's claim that the Negro will give Western Civilization the spiritual dynamic it so badly needs.

KING SAY HE HOPE THE SPIRITUAL POWER OF THE NEGRO CAN RADIATE OUT TO THE WORLD AND CHALLENGE THE NATIONS OF THE WORLD TO HIGHER GROUND.

THIS IS HEADY STUFF.

A CHOSEN PEOPLE SCENARIO TRYING TO AVOID THE CHOSEN PEOPLE SYNDROME BY ROOTING IT IN A VISION OF SERVICE.

This what bring King to a vision of blackfolk as a folk with a destiny.

THIS WHAT MOVE HIM TO THE PROPHETIC.

VISITS TO AFRICA AND INDIA SOLIDIFY HIS GLOBAL VISION.

Ghana, he is Nkrumah's guest at his inauguration as president of the 1st African country to achieve independence. King realize now there is a world full of black people to serve.

India, he walk around New Delhi in a Gandhi cap, following in the footsteps of his idol, his mentor in struggle. He identify with the Untouchables and is impressed by India's affirmative action program, with Gandhi's attempt to give them dignity. Children of God indeed.

HE IS FURTHER REINFORCED IN HIS OWN BELIEF IN NONVIOLENCE AS A VIABLE STRATEGY.

"SINC
MORE
BEFO
NONW
THE M
AVAIL
PEOP
JUSTI
IN A R
GAND
CERTA
THAT
MORA
VERS
ARE A
LAW C

EING IN INDIA, I AM
ONVINCED THAN EVER
THAT THE METHOD OF
LENT RESISTANCE IS
T POTENT WEAPON
LE TO OPPRESSED
N THEIR STRUGGLE FOR
AND HUMAN DIGNITY.
L SENSE, MAHATMA
EMBODIED IN HIS LIFE
UNIVERSAL PRINCIPLES
E INHERENT IN THE
STRUCTURE OF THE UNI-
ND THESE PRINCIPLES
NESCAPABLE AS THE
GRAVITATION."

He resolves upon returning home to be more like Gandhi. First thing he do is set a day aside for meditation and reflection.

YOU KNOW ABOUT HOW LONG THAT LAST.

THINGS TO DO. PEOPLE TO SEE.

KING ACCEPT THAT HE IS NOT THE MOST DISCI-PLINED OF HOLYMEN.

Round about this time he decide he need a bigger stage. He leave Montgomery and return to Atlanta.

JUST IN TIME FOR HIS NEXT BIG CHALLENGE. ALBANY, GEORGIA.

THE ALBANY MOVEMENT 1961

NOVEMBER OF 1961

THE ALBANY MOVEMENT IS FORMED BY LOCAL ACTIVISTS IN ALBANY, GEORGIA.

1000s OF BLACKS ARE MOBILIZED IN A BROAD-BASED ASSAULT ON SEGREGATION PRACTICES.

DECEMBER 1961, KING IS INVITED IN.

He decide he can spare a day for them but is arrested in a mass sweep and sentenced to jail. King refuses bail until city makes concessions he accept as a win but when Albany doesn't follow through on its promises he returns.

He is arrested again but understanding now the value of being incarcerated he once again refuses bail. The police chief, an equally perceptive fellow, surreptitiously pays his bail.

KING SAY HE'S BEEN THROWN OFF BUSES AND OUT OF LUNCH COUNTERS BUT THIS IS THE 1ST TIME HE'S EVER BEEN THROWN OUT OF JAIL.

After almost a year of struggle, dissension and a refusal by the powers that be to engage in mediaworthy violence the campaign's energy is sapped and SCLC withdraws in a defeat, pregnant with lessons learned and new strategies.

–strategy is to force confrontations with violent authorities and shame America by generating media coverage that force the government to act against the evident evils of Southern apartheid.

The Southern position is that blacks are happy and comfortable with the system as it is

AND TOO MANY AMERICANS BELIEVE THIS TO BE SO.

MLK IS DETERMINED TO SHOW THE LIE OF THAT.

ALBANY IS COUNTED AS ONE OF HIS FAILURES, BUT FAILURES CAN BE USEFUL TOO.

Albany supply lessons King apply to Birmingham.

BIRMINGHAM:

THE CHILDREN'S CRUSADE 1963

It was Fred Shuttlesworth ask King into Birmingham. Spring of 1963 they commence a protest campaign. When Birmingham refuse to desegregate, SCLC implement Wyatt T. Walker's strategy of civil disobedience. Project C.

STRATEGY IS FILL THE JAILS AND PROVOKE THE AUTHORITIES INTO MEDIAWORTHY REPRESSION.

TELEVISION STILL A RELATIVELY NEW MEDIUM THEN

(APPARENTLY THE REVOLUTION WILL BE TELEVISED, YOUTUBED, FACEBOOKED, ET AL.)

AND KING IS A PAST MASTER AT USING EVOLVING TECHNOLOGY AS STRATEGY.

HE IS ALSO ADEPT AT CLASSIC IDEOLOGICAL TECHNOLOGY

–arrested again and with a keen sense of the historical moment, King uses his time in jail to pen Letter from Birmingham Jail. It is a classic jailhouse manifesto, historical in its scope.

ALL HIS BOOKS WORTH READING. ONGOING ACCOUNT OF HIS STRATEGIC EVOLUTION.

Bull Connor's strategy is arrest them all and soon enough SCLC had run out of bodies.

SOMEBODY SUGGEST USING THE CHILDREN.

THIS IS A CONTROVERSIAL SUGGESTION. THE DANGER SOME SAY.

BUT THE NEXT DAY IT IS THE CHILDREN TAKING TO THE STREETS OF BIRMINGHAM.

MARCHING AND SINGING THE FREEDOM SONGS.

AIN'T GONNA LET NOBODY TURN ME AROUND. TURN ME AROUND.

The children of Birmingham. Marching on the frontlines.

IT IS A SIGHT TO WARM THE SOUL.

AMERICA IS SHOCKED.
SHOCKED I TELL YOU.

This is more than the national consciousness (and local power brokers) can bear.

BIRMINGHAM CAPITULATES.

KING IS THE MAN AFTER BIRMINGHAM. BLACK AMERICA'S ACKNOWLEDGED LEADER.

MANY OF KING'S DEMANDS ARE BROUGHT TO FRUITION IN THE CIVIL RIGHTS ACT OF 1964 AND THE VOTING RIGHTS ACT OF 1965.

Wherever he go he cause downtrodden blackfolk to believe in themselves and take action designed to alleviate their condition,

NO MATTER THE DIFFICULTY, NO MATTER THE DANGER.

HE INSPIRE THEM LIKE NO OTHER SINCE OR BEFORE.

CAP IT ALL WITH THE MARCH ON WASHINGTON.

KING'S SHINING HOUR.

A COALITION OF CIVIL RIGHTS ORGANIZATIONS DECIDE TO MARCH ON WASHINGTON TO PUBLICIZE THE STRUGGLE AND DEMAND GOVERNMENT ACTION.

It is the largest gathering of protestors in the nation's history.

A SPEECH THAT DEFINE THE MOMENT, AND FOR MANY, THE ERA.

KING IS AT THE TOP OF HIS GAME. THESE ARE THE YEARS OF HIS TRIUMPHS.

BIRMINGHAM,

THE MARCH ON WASHINGTON,

THE NOBEL PEACE PRIZE,

TIME'S MAN OF THE YEAR.

He on speaking terms with the powers that be and he basking in the adulation of the people. Got a loving wife and a growing family, got a vision –

ALL THE GOOD THINGS IN LIFE.

These of course are the years the Gods begin to extract the payment they always require of greatness.

Now that he The Man, new forces rise in the black community to challenge him as he had himself once challenged the old guard.

HIS CHALLENGE IS PERSONIFIED IN MALCOLM X, SELLING A VISION OF PRIDE AND VIGILANCE AND AN EYE FOR AN EYE VIOLENCE

THAT ANGRY BLACKFOLK FIND MIGHTY TEMPTING.

THE RISE OF MALCOLM REINFORCE KING'S DETERMINATION TO TRACK TO THE HIGHROAD.

NOT ONLY DOES HE SINCERELY BELIEVE IN THE MORAL IMPERATIVE OF NONVIOLENCE,

THE PANTHERS CHOSE THAT OPTION;

YOU SEE WHAT HAPPEN TO THEM.

HE IS DETERMINED THAT IT WOULD NOT,

COULD NOT, COME TO THAT.

But where he had assured the old guard there were many roads to Timbuktu, now that he himself is challenged, he realize it's not that simple. To the old guard, new ways are often perceived not only as wrong, but dangerous.

KING'S PRIMARY CONCERN IS THAT BLACK PEOPLE NOT BECOME EMBITTERED BY STRUGGLE BUT ILLUMINATED.

HE CONSIDER THE STRUGGLE MOST FUNDA-MENTALLY ONE FOR THE SOULS OF BLACKFOLK.

BUT ALL AROUND HIM THE STRUGGLE GOING HARDCORE.

RIOTS HAVE STRUCK THE CITIES, PEOPLE HAVE DIED.

In the philosophy of Malcolm, the Panthers, Black Power and the riots, Martin detect bitterness and frustration taking root in the African American soul. The very thing he has tried to finesse.

GAINING THE NOBEL PEACE PRIZE IS PERHAPS THE PEAK OF HIS POWER, THE YOUNGEST PERSON EVER AWARDED IT.

HE IS HUMBLED BY THE EXPERIENCE, BUT IT CAN'T HELP BUT BROADEN HIS VISION OF HIMSELF AND THE HISTORICAL ROLE HE PLAYING.

It is at this point that he consciously couple the Black Struggle with the Struggle for Human Dignity.

"WE MUST FOREVER C
STRUGGLE ON THE HIG
AND DISCIPLINE."

WHAT HE SAYING HER
COME TO THE CROSSR
THE HIGHROAD. ALWA
GREATER THAN YOU A

But it is winning the Nobel Peace Prize that infuriate
his most implacable foe, J. Edgar Hoover of the FBI.
After his I Have A Dream speech, Hoover call King

"THE MOST DANGERO
NEGRO LEADER IN TH
EVEN BETTER, "THAT
PREACHER."

ONDUCT OUR
H PLANE OF DIGNITY

IS WHENEVER YOU
OADS, ALWAYS TAKE
S STRIVE TO BE
RE.

S AND EFFECTIVE
COUNTRY."
ODDAMNED NIGGER

NOW

PERSONALLY, I WOULDN'T MIND BEING CALLED THE MOST EFFECTIVE NEGRO LEADER IN THE COUNTRY,

BUT HOOVER CONSIDER THIS MORE OF AN INSULT THAN GODDAMN NIGGER PREACHER.

Using allegations of communist influence he convince AG Bobby Kennedy to authorize wiretaps on King.

This allegation of communist influence come from Southern barons convinced their Negroes are happy and satisfied Negroes. Had to be outside agitators riling their Negroes up like this.

HOOVER DIDN'T GET ANY EVIDENCE OF COMMUNIST INFLUENCE BUT HE DID GET SEX TAPES.

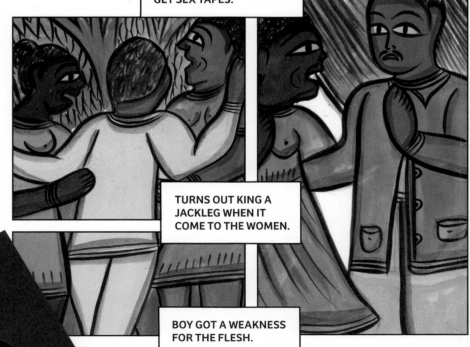

TURNS OUT KING A JACKLEG WHEN IT COME TO THE WOMEN.

BOY GOT A WEAKNESS FOR THE FLESH.

So, Hoover got all this juicy agonizing on tape and when King is chosen for the Nobel, Hoover send the tape to the King household with a note

SOME CONTEND ENCOURAGE KING TO COMMIT SUICIDE.

Nonetheless, those early years, those early campaigns –nothing but victories–but that doesn't make for a very interesting story does it–it's defeat that season the soul.

WELL, AT LEAST THE GODS
ARE PLEASED. IN FACT
THEY RATHER TICKLED.

THIS INSTRUMENT HAS
BEEN ALL WE COULD ASK
FOR, SAY THE GODS.

LET US NOW TEST HIM.

LET US SEND HIM TO ST.
AUGUSTINE. LET US SEE
WHAT HE MADE OF.

SELMA AND SAINT AUGUSTINE: THE STING OF DEFEAT

1964, local activists
in St. Augustine, Florida,
begin a campaign of civil
disobedience.

Same same Selma, Dec. '64, marchers obey an injunction that saps their momentum and again, defeat and withdrawal. The powers that be have learned how to counter his strategies.

MEANWHILE THE MOVEMENT HAS GROWN MORE COMPLEX ON HIM.

IMPATIENT WITH THE PASSIVITY OF NONVIOLENCE, THE YOUNG TURKS HAVE BEGUN TO TURN THEIR BACKS ON KING AND HIS NONVIOLENCE TOO.

This is exemplified in his troubled relationship with SNCC. The Student Nonviolent Coordinating Committee had been founded with his help and nurtured by SCLC in its infancy. King is dismayed when they accuse him of being an Uncle Tom.

(ACTUALLY UNCLE TOM HAS GOTTEN A BAD RAP. CHECK THE TEXT, HE WASN'T THAT BAD. DID WHAT HE COULD WITH WHAT HE HAD. WASN'T NO GUNGA DIN.)

SOME IN SCLC BEGAN TO QUESTION ITS RELIANCE ON MARCHES.

VOTERS' REGISTRATION IS WHERE THE ACTION IS.

The Kennedy boys, hoping to blunt black activism with electoral politics and pressure the Southern barons, supporting it. The people want it, SNCC riding it. Better late than never, SCLC gets on board.

MISSISSIPPI FREEDOM SUMMER AND BLOODY SUNDAY: SELMA 1965

When SNCC decide to take voters' registration activists into rural Mississippi, King and the SCLC advise against it,

> TOO DANGEROUS GOING OFF IN THOSE MISSISSIPPI BACKWOODS, THEY WARN.

SNCC, with the invincibility of youth, go into rural Mississippi anyway and the South respond with night riders and vigilante violence. Schwerner, Chaney and Goodman snatched out their cars and tossed into unmarked graves.

> BLACKS DARE REGISTER TO VOTE BOMBED, KILLED, FIRED, TOSSED OFF THE LAND.

> THE MISSISSIPPI FREEDOM SUMMER CAN BE CONSIDERED A SUCCESSFUL CAMPAIGN.

> O BUT THE COST.

IT ALL COME TO A HEAD ON BLOODY SUNDAY.

When SNCC and locals decide on a march from Selma to Montgomery, King advise against it and doesn't participate. Mob meet March at the Pettus Bridge. TV does it again, and the nation is riveted. How can this be.

King organize a new march but stops it at the Pettus Bridge. This infuriate SNCC and the locals. Once again King accused of being a sellout. The young Turks have taken to calling him "De Lawd," the saintly fellow from the movie, Green Pastures.

KING IS MORTALLY WOUNDED BY THIS.

AFTER ALL I'VE DONE HE PROTEST.

AFTER ALL I'VE GIVEN.

Stokely Carmichael replace James Farmer Jr., as chair of SNCC. When James Meredith shot during his solitary March Against Fear, King, Stokely and others gather to continue it.

112

Watts and Newark got him reeling, burn baby burn, King feel the struggle slipping away from him. Driven by a need to regain lost ground, an expanding sense of his historical mission, the nagging call of Fa and a ministry that has begun to perceive poverty a violence as unjust as segregation,

KING MAKES DECISION TO NATION-ALIZE THE STRUGGLE AND ATTACK THE CONDITION OF BLACKS IN THE NORTHERN GHETTOS.

LIKE SO MANY SOUTHERN BLACK MIGRANTS, KING DECIDE TO TAKE ON CHICAGO.

SWEET HOME CHICAGO; SORRY BUT I CAN'T TAKE YOU 1966

To move on Chicago, SCLC ally with the Coordinating Council of Community Organization. King and Abernathy open the campaign with a little revolutionary theater – moving their families into the Lawndale slum, nailing his manifesto to the doors of City Hall. Test couples are sent out on housing discrimination missions, marches are sent into the ethnic enclaves of Chicago.

THIS BECOMES A REVELATION.

THE PASSION OF THE PROTESTORS SURPRISE THEM,

A HATRED, CLAIM ABERNATHY, WORSE THAN THAT OF THE SOUTH.

Between mob violence and Daley's machine politic, King is stymied in Chicago. Had that country boy spinning his wheels. After seeding Jesse Jackson and Operation Breadbasket, SCLC implement a strategic withdrawal, humbled and humiliated.

BLACK POWER ON ONE SIDE,

KING UNDER THE GUN NOW,

WHITE INTRANSIGENCE ON THE OTHER

AND A STRING OF CRIPPLING DEFEATS IN BETWEEN.

YOU CAN TELL HE FEELING HIS MORTALITY WHEN YOU LISTEN TO THE DRUMMAJOR SPEECH HE GAVE WHEN HE RETURN TO EBENEZER.

GOT UP TO THE PULPIT AND HE PAUSE SO LONG THE CONGREGATION BEGIN TO WONDER. GOT THEIR FULL ATTENTION WHEN HE FINALLY SPEAK.

SAY WHEN IT COME TIM
TELL THE PREACHER N
HE TELL THEM DON'T V
ON MY AWARDS (WHIC
LOVINGLY LIST). HE TE
TO REMEMBER THAT M
TRIED TO FEED THE HU
TO CLOTHE THE NAKE
BE RIGHT ON THE WAR
THEM MARTIN LUTHER
AND SERVE HUMANITY
DRUMMAJOR, A DRUM

TO GIVE HIS EULOGY,
TO TALK TOO LONG.
STE YOUR TIME
HE THEN RATHER
THEM I WANT YOU
RTIN LUTHER KING
GRY. THAT I TRIED
HAT I TRIED TO
UESTION. TELL
NG TRIED TO LOVE
AY THAT I WAS A
AJOR FOR JUSTICE.

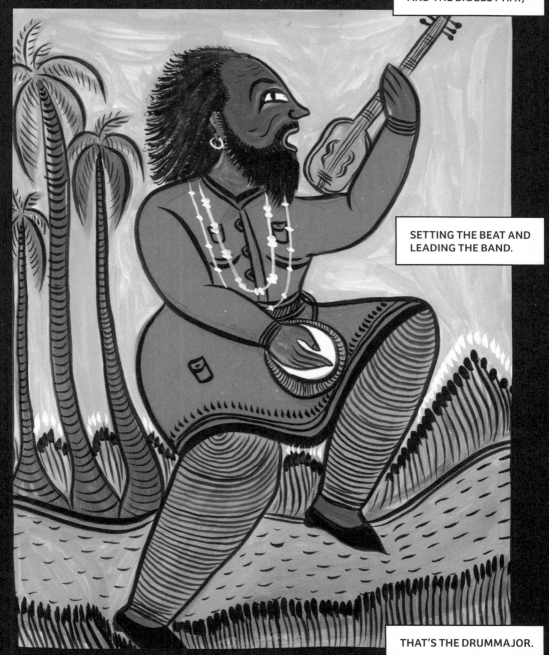

GOT THE BEST UNIFORM AND THE BIGGEST HAT,

SETTING THE BEAT AND LEADING THE BAND.

THAT'S THE DRUMMAJOR.

Old allies from Roy Wilkins to LBJ turn on him and the once adoring media pillory him, liberals, conservatives, blacks and whites,

THEY ALL TELL HIM TO MIND HIS OWN BUSINESS,

SAY MARTIN LUTHER KING DON'T KNOW WHAT HE TALKING ABOUT. BEST HE STICK TO WHAT HE KNOW BEST.

COLORED PEOPLE.

BUT KING JUST DIDN'T SEE NO WAY HE COULD AVOID CALLING IT FOR WHAT IT WAS—AN UNJUST WAR. A STAIN ON AMERICA'S SOUL.

For King it boil down to the right thing to do: "Cowardice asks the question—is it safe? Expediency asks the question—is it politic? Vanity asks the question—is it popular? But conscience asks the question—is it right?

And there comes a time when one must take a position that is neither safe, nor politic, nor popular;

BUT ONE MUST TAKE IT BECAUSE IT IS RIGHT."

HE HAS BEGUN TO DOUBT HIMSELF. MAYBE MALCOM RIGHT. MAYBE I'M WRONG. MAYBE MY TIME HAS PASSED.

OLD BOY FEELING UNAPPRECIATED.

WHY IS HE STILL DOING THIS. HE CAN'T COME UP WITH A CONVINCING ANSWER.

EXCEPT THIS WHAT HE DO. NOBODY ELSE CAN DO WHAT HE DO.

Look how far we've come, Martin. Now is not the time to get weary, Martin. Look all what still need to be done.

IN WHAT IS
ALMOST AN ACT
OF DESPERATION

KING DECIDE ON
THE POOR PEOPLE'S
CAMPAIGN.

They would challenge the government to implement a Bill
of Rights. For all poor people. All of them. Black, white,
whatever. Fullcourt campaign of civil disobedience. Fill
the federal jails. Force the government to act.

His advisors advise against it. In the past campaigns have
been designed to bring the federal government into the
fray on their side. This one would be designed to challenge
the federal government itself.

NOT SMART, MARTIN.

BUT KING INSIST.
HIS ADVISORS DUTIFULLY BEGIN
THEIR PREPARATIONS WHEN
ONCE AGAIN HE IS CALLED UPON
BY THE HARD HAND OF DESTINY.

IT CAN BE ARGUED THAT MEMPHIS SAVED KING. HE WAS IN DECLINE, HIS MOVES REEKED OF DESPERATION, THE STRUGGLE HAD MOVED ON WITHOUT HIM.

MEMPHIS TOOK HIM OUT AT THE TOP OF HIS GAME AND ENSURED HIS LEGACY. WHAT MORE CAN A PLAYER ASK.

For some years now he has soldiered on in spite of increasing doubts. He has learned the true lesson of leadership–you always pay more than you get–real leadership always cost. Misstep don't just cost you, it cost the people who believe in you. Depending on you.

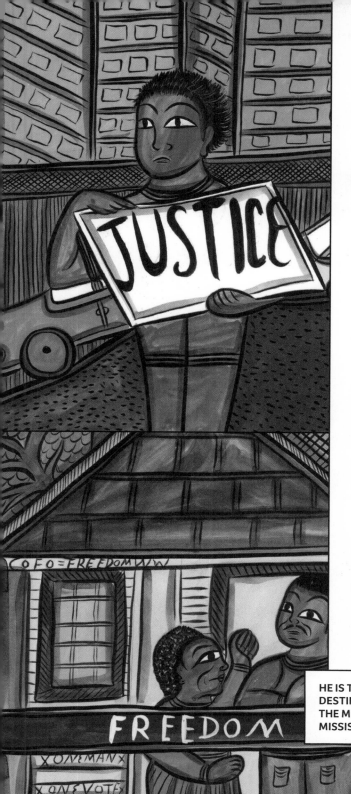

When King was once accused of being an agitator he replied

— I AM HERE BECAUSE

THERE ARE TWENTY MILLION NEGROES IN THE UNITED STATES AND I LOVE EVERY ONE OF THEM.

The Gods have actually been rather pleased with his service. But it is difficult to satisfy the Gods for long. There is one more thing they would ask of him and so they send him to Memphis.

HE IS TO MEET HIS FA THERE. DESTINY AWAIT HIM ON THE MUDDY BANKS OF THE MISSISSIPPI RIVER.

MEET ME ON THE MOUNTAIN TOP, I'VE SEEN THE PROMISELAND.

MEMPHIS 1968

March of 1968, a strike by sanitation workers has polarized Memphis and local leaders ask King to lend a hand.

Preoccupied with preparation for his Poor People's March, King reluctantly decide he can spare a day or so to help old Memphis colleagues in struggle. He flies in to participate in a march already organized by local activists.

QUICK IN QUICK OUT, THAT'S THE PLAN.

BUT THE MARCH IS DISRUPTED BY LOCAL MILITANTS, THE INVADERS.

A RIOT ERUPT AND A 16 YEAR OLD IS KILLED. KING IS DEVASTATED. HE HAS NEVER LOST A MARCHER.

THE MEDIA AND HIS ENEMIES INSIST THIS PROVES ONCE AND FOR ALL THAT HIS VAUNTED NONVIOLENCE IS AN EMPTY VESSEL,

THAT HE IS NO LONGER A VIABLE LEADER,

MUCH LESS THE LEADER.

KING TAKES THIS PERSONAL.

HE RESOLVE TO TRY AGAIN, THIS TIME WITH HIS OWN ORGANIZERS.

So, April 3rd, he return to Memphis. Evening before the march there is a big storm out of the Gulf and Memphis is lashed with hurricane work–thunder and lightning and stormbent trees. King, tired and dispirited, decide surely no one would show for the big rally planned that evening at the Mason Temple. He send Abernathy in his place.

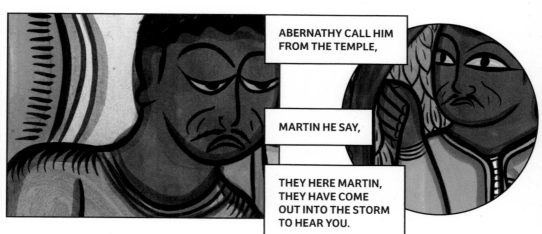

ABERNATHY CALL HIM FROM THE TEMPLE,

MARTIN HE SAY,

THEY HERE MARTIN, THEY HAVE COME OUT INTO THE STORM TO HEAR YOU.

King try to beg off, surely you can handle it Ralph, but Abernathy insist,

NO MARTIN, IT'S YOU THEY'VE COME OUT INTO THE STORM TO HEAR,

IT'S YOU THEY'VE COME TO SEE.

AND SO KING DON HIS ARMOR THIS ONE LAST TIME AND HE GO ON OVER TO THE TEMPLE.

Now, let me tell you, you had to actually be there that night to really appreciate this. Nothing I can say will bring this to life for you like it actually was.

YOU GOT A STORM OF MYTHIC
PROPORTION LASHING AT THE
BUILDING AND KING AT THE TOP
OF HIS GAME.

SOME SAY HE KNEW IT WAS COMING,
THAT 30 ODD 6 BULLET.

SOME WILL POINT OUT THAT HE HAS
USED THESE BITS OF RHETORIC BEFORE,
THAT THE THREAT OF ASSASSINATION
WAS HIS CONSTANT COMPANION,

THAT HE HAS LONG SINCE MADE
HIS PEACE WITH DEATH.

Was it Chicago that black woman stab him in the chest. Left a pair of scissors a sneeze away from his heart.

THE DOCTOR CUT THOSE SCISSORS OUT OF HIS CHEST LEFT A SCAR IN THE SHAPE OF A CROSS.

SAY HE FOUND IT SOMEHOW FITTING,

and sometime when King feeling his mortality he finger that raised flesh on his chest. Now, I believe he knew myself. I believe he knew his day had come. I heard it in his voice, the way he choose his words.

LISTEN TO THE TAPE IF YOU DON'T BELIEVE ME.

THIS THE NIGHT THAT HE SPOKE IN TONGUES.

"WELL, I DON'T KNOW W
WE'VE GOT SOME DIFFIC
IT DOESN'T MATTER WIT
I'VE BEEN TO THE MOUN
MIND. LIKE ANYBODY, I V
A LONG LIFE. LONGEVIT
I'M NOT CONCERNED AB
WANT TO DO GOD'S WIL
ME TO GO UP TO THE MC
LOOKED OVER. AND I'VE
LAND. I MAY NOT GET TI
WANT YOU TO KNOW TO
PEOPLE, WILL GET TO TI

HAT WILL HAPPEN NOW.
ULT DAYS AHEAD. BUT
H ME NOW. BECAUSE
TAINTOP. AND I DON'T
OULD LIKE TO LIVE
HAS ITS PLACE. BUT
OUT THAT NOW. I JUST
AND HE'S ALLOWED
UNTAIN. AND I'VE
SEEN THE PROMISED
ERE WITH YOU. BUT I
IGHT, THAT WE, AS A
E PROMISED LAND."

NEXT DAY A 30–06 TOOK OFF HIS JAW

AND CLEAVED HIS SPINE.

THIS THE PROMISE HE MADE. STAMPED PAID IN BLOOD.

There are certain public events in your life you remember where you were when you heard the news. I heard it over the car radio.

MARTIN LUTHER KING HAS BEEN SHOT.

I wonder sometime about his legacy. I know he did. I know he wondered sometime if it was worth it all.

Wondered sometime why me. But he accepted the deal the Gods offer the chosen with a full heart. My understanding is that his last words were to musician Ben Branch of Operation Breadbasket:

BEN,

MAKE SURE YOU PLAY TAKE MY HAND, PRECIOUS LORD IN THE MEETING TONIGHT.

PLAY IT REAL PRETTY.

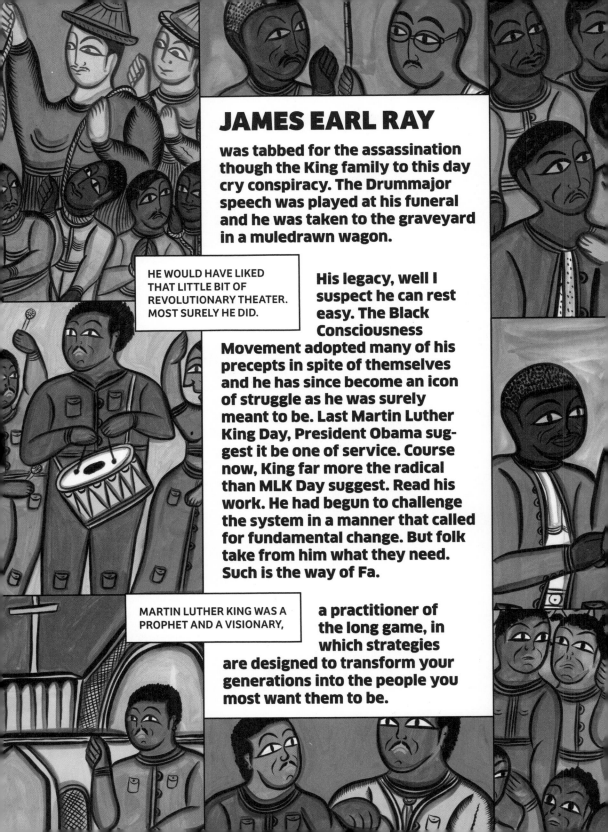

JAMES EARL RAY

was tabbed for the assassination though the King family to this day cry conspiracy. The Drummajor speech was played at his funeral and he was taken to the graveyard in a muledrawn wagon.

HE WOULD HAVE LIKED THAT LITTLE BIT OF REVOLUTIONARY THEATER. MOST SURELY HE DID.

His legacy, well I suspect he can rest easy. The Black Consciousness Movement adopted many of his precepts in spite of themselves and he has since become an icon of struggle as he was surely meant to be. Last Martin Luther King Day, President Obama suggest it be one of service. Course now, King far more the radical than MLK Day suggest. Read his work. He had begun to challenge the system in a manner that called for fundamental change. But folk take from him what they need. Such is the way of Fa.

MARTIN LUTHER KING WAS A PROPHET AND A VISIONARY,

a practitioner of the long game, in which strategies are designed to transform your generations into the people you most want them to be.

So many names to be added to the Great Black Book of Generations – Bob Moses; Fannie Lou Hamer; the Five Saints of Birmingham; Babajohn Killens, the Great Griot Master of Brooklyn – soldiers too many to mention. This is a generation that can be proud of its contribution. This is a generation rich in Fa.

And proudest of all. Martin Luther King. May your works endure. May they serve many generations.

I AM RICKYDOC TRICKMASTER. I HAVE BEEN CALLED TO WITNESS. CLEAR AS DAY I RECALL HIM THAT NIGHT AT THE TEMPLE, SWEAT BEADING THAT GREAT MOON OF A FACE. I KNOW HE FELT THE POWER THEN. HE SHOWERED US IN ITS GRACE.

IT IS NOT EASY TO BE AN INSTRUMENT OF THE GODS.

DUES MUST BE PAID. BURDENS BORNE.

But I'm told the life well-spent is one of service. I'm told that Martin Luther King, in his short life, became the face of struggle that changed our lives. The Civil War may have delivered the blacks from slavery, but it was Martin Luther King delivered us from bondage.

EDITORIAL NOTES, IN CHRONOLOGICAL ORDER

BAPTIST CHURCHES

Baptist churches in the American South have both supported as well as contested slavery. Exclusive African American churches existed from as early as the eighteenth century – and through the difficult years of slavery nurtured community life. Baptist preachers emerged as community leaders, encouraged education and fostered dignity and confidence. These churches played an important role in inspiring African Americans to challenge racial discrimination and helped build the movement for civil rights.

AMERICAN CIVIL WAR

Also known as the War of the States, the American Civil War lasted for four years (1861–65). It was the result of increasing political tension between the slave-holding Southern states and the increasingly anti-slavery Northern states. When the free states of the North sought to arrest the spread of slavery, powerful slave owners in the South felt threatened and got their state governments to secede from the American Union, precipitating a civil war.

RECONSTRUCTION

When Northern troops occupied the South during the American Civil War, African American slaves began to desert plantations and other places of work, forcing President Lincoln to issue the Emancipation Proclamation in 1863. Lincoln also wanted the labor 'freed' from slavery for the army of the North. However, hungry for freedom and land, former slaves looked forward to building a new society in the South. At the same time, reform-minded people in the Northern states called for re-building social and political life. These events presaged the coming of the Reconstruction era during which questions to do with the rights of former slaves were debated. This period ended formally in 1877 with white Americans re-establishing their supremacy in the South.

KU KLUX KLAN

Founded in 1865 by people who believed in white supremacy, the Klan used intimidation and murder to restore white power. Though banned during the Reconstruction era, the Klan re-emerged in subsequent decades to proclaim its politics of hate and violence – first in the 1920s, and later during the 1960s, which witnessed African Americans' fight for civil rights. The burning cross was a distinctive symbol of the Ku Klux Klan during its active second phase, in the 1920s.

BLACK CODES

As the Reconstruction era ended, several Southern states passed laws known as Black Codes – in 1865 and 1866 – to regulate and control the labor and mobility of newly freed slaves. The infamous Jim Crow laws, enacted in 1877, further legitimized racist segregation and discrimination. The Civil Rights Legislation of 1964 and the Voting Rights Act of 1965 effectively ended the tyranny of these unworthy laws.

BROWN VS BOARD OF EDUCATION

Oliver L. Brown – a welder and pastor – and 12 other individuals filed a case in the local district court in Kansas protesting the segregation of public schools. The court upheld segregation and the matter went up to the US Supreme Court, where a landmark judgment overturned the district court's verdict and declared segregation unconstitutional in 1954.

NAACP

The National Association for the Advancement of Colored People is one of America's oldest civil rights groups. It was formed in 1909 by a diverse group of people, including reformist white Americans, and took up a number of issues, including the widespread lynching of African American men in the American South, segregation and the denial of full civil rights to people of color.

URBAN LEAGUE

Following the Great Migration northward, former slaves discovered that all was not well in the cities they came to inhabit. Soon committees were set up to assist urban African Americans, including workers and women. These various committees merged to form the National League on Urban Conditions Among Negroes in 1910. Subsequently, this came to be known as the National Urban League.

FRED SHUTTLESWORTH

A civil rights activist and pastor, Shuttlesworth co-founded the Southern Christian Leadership Conference – the SCLC – and also the Alabama Christian Movement for Human Rights. A close associate of Martin Luther King Jr., he continued to be active in civil rights work until 2006. He died in 2011.

WYATT T WALKER; PROJECT C

A highly respected civil rights leader and pastor, Walker was Martin Luther King Jr.'s veritable Chief of Staff in his various civil rights marches. Along with Fred Shuttlesworth, he initiated Project C – C for 'Confrontation' – which was a strategic plan for mass marches in Birmingham, Alabama. He lead from the front, and was arrested 17 times.

BULL CONNOR

Chief of Police in Birmingham, Alabama, in the 1960s, Eugene 'Bull' Connor was brutally against racial integration. He was infamously associated with such acts as using police attack dogs and fire hoses against African American protest marchers.

OPERATION BREADBASKET

Operation Breadbasket was launched by the SCLC in Atlanta, in 1962, to persuade businesses patronized by black people to hire more members of the black community. Breadbasket made it clear that black people would boycott businesses that did not have fair hiring practices.

SCHWERNER, CHANEY, GOODMAN

In 1964, Michael Schwerner, a social worker, James Chaney, an African American worker, and Andrew Goodman, a white Jewish student, were lynched by members of the Ku Klux Klan in Mississippi, as they campaigned to get African Americans to register for voting in the elections.

THE KENNEDY BOYS

President John F. Kennedy's brother, US Attorney General Robert Kennedy, was involved in the civil rights movement in the 1960s. While broadly endorsing Martin Luther King Jr.'s politics, Robert Kennedy and his men warned him to stay clear of communism and communists. Robert Kennedy also attempted to steer King in the direction of electoral politics.

PANTHERS

The Black Panther Party of the USA was founded in 1966 by Huey P. Newton. Associated with militant socialism and black nationalism, the Panthers confronted police brutality directly and sometimes violently. Concerned with the safety of African American neighborhoods, the Panthers organized watch committees to monitor police behavior. While the Panthers attracted a diverse following, their violent approach to politics also earned them criticism from within the community.

BLACK POWER

This was a term coined by Stokely Carmichael that came to stand for black political confidence and autonomy as well as solidarity among black people.

BLACK PRIDE

This term is associated with various ideas of pride and cultural consciousness on the part of people of African descent. Particularly resonant for African Americans in the 1960s and 1970s, it served as a rallying cry for black collective interests.

WHITE FREEDOM SUMMER VETS (VETERANS)

In the summer of 1964, a number of white liberals and supporters of desegregation marched to Mississippi to participate in the great voter registration campaigns organized by the Student Nonviolent Coordinating Committee. Following the violence in the wake of the campaign, Black Power slogans gained the day. In 1967, the SNCC expelled its white staff and volunteers, including those who had marched alongside them in the Freedom Summer of 1964.

WATTS, NEWARK

Watts in Los Angeles, California, and Newark in New Jersey, home to thousands of poor African Americans, witnessed violent racial riots in the 1960s due to poor housing, poverty and racial discrimination.

DALEY'S MACHINE POLITIC

Richard Daley was the mayor of Chicago when Martin Luther King Jr. took up residence in that city and sought to organize protests and marches. Daley's political presence and organizational power did not quite serve King's purpose and thwarted his labors.

CONVERSATIONS ACROSS CULTURES

This book has a long and unusual story. It began as a set of painted panels at a workshop we organized with Patua artists, traditional scroll painters from Bengal. An essentially pre-literate, oral folk practice, the Patua tradition is a mixture of performance, storytelling and art. The story is recited or sung as the narrator holds up the scroll and points to an illustrative image. Unlike many other narrative folk-art forms – where the entire action is condensed within one frame – Patua images are read sequentially. Given the way they unfold, we wanted to try an exciting experiment: why not nudge them towards, the form of a contemporary graphic novel?

Patua artists have their own repertoire of traditional tales. But they also love new stories, and will quickly and fearlessly make them their own. One of the narratives we selected for the workshop was the inspiring story of Martin Luther King Jr. We didn't have our own version of it yet, but came up with the bare bones of the plot, translated into Bangla. Manu Chitrakar, one of the artists, was immediately keen to try his hand at it. He had never heard of Martin Luther King Jr., nor was he familiar with the history of slavery, racism or the civil rights movement. But he still related to the story in a deeply felt way. Sadly, social injustice is universal, though it takes particular forms: India has its own caste system, with people deemed 'untouchable' at the very bottom; to be in economic and social bondage to a richer and more powerful man was also common enough in Manu's own world.

Manu grasped these connections intuitively, and was keen to translate King's story into his own idiom and ways of rendering. The reader will notice that a number of Manu's figures are iconic, tending to be serene in both pain and happiness. This is a stylistic trope, part of his inherited tradition, and it allows for a certain collective inclusiveness. At the same time, there is another – curiously transcendent and allusive – way in which Patua artists integrate the new into their world. Manu was keen to see actual pictures from the period our story was set in, but in his own final images, his African Americans wear Indian saris and dhotis, carry Bangla signs, and are poor and bonded in a typically Indian fashion. This is his way of owning the story, of making it resonate in his own context. Entirely unselfconsciously, in the process, it also becomes universal.

While Manu was working on his initial set of images, something serendipitous happened. We met Arthur Flowers – African American writer and griot – at a literature festival in India, and asked whether he would be interested in writing the text for our book. We thought it would be a good match, but had no idea just how unexpected and creative the dialogue would turn out to be. Arthur's engagement with the subject was intense and personal. It was a theme he had been wanting to take on for a long time, and he had himself been an active participant in the civil rights movement. We sent him Manu's images, and he started to write. The text he finally sent us was extraordinary – lyrical and fabular, resounding with the cadences of oral storytelling from an altogether different tradition.

This text called for more, and different, images. We worked with Manu once again, and this time around, he wasn't just illustrating events, but creating visual metaphors for a layered tale. Manu enjoyed this challenge, imaginatively crossing over into a new realm of storytelling. He came up with ever more brilliant transversions: turning Arthur's bandleader into a mystic Bengali Baul singer and placing the Ku Klux Klan strategically in places he thought appropriate. His final vision of the Promised Land culminates in a solidarity that is truly poignant: King stretches out his arms in prophetic majesty, embracing not just his own people, but the image of an Indian idyll.

Yet our project was still not done. We needed another voice: a designer to enable a successful dialogue between the text and images, within the pages of a book. This was when we brought young Italian designer Guglielmo Rossi into the story. His challenge was to create a conversation between two singular voices – two cultures, in more ways than one – by giving each one its due, while making them speak together for the reader. It was a very novel and complex brief, given the tangentiality of the relationship between the two. Guglielmo has worked with type in several ways: the magisterial voice of King's mighty speeches is treated differently from opinion, argument and commentary. He crops and sequences images both illustratively, in relation to the text, but also wordlessly, narrating the broad sweep of history in a manner that hints at their scroll ancestry. He came up with the final form of the book as it stands now.

But that is still not the end of the story, or at least not the end of this rich and many-sided conversation, which has now meandered into the curious by-lanes of cultural exchange: While he was working on this book with us, Manu Chitrakar painted his own scroll of the Martin Luther King Jr. story, which began to circulate among the Patuas, becoming a part of their repertoire. Manu painted a scroll for Arthur as well, who now uses it in North America, Patua-style, when he performs his story.

Gita Wolf
V. Geetha
Tara Books

PATUA GRAPHICS

This graphic novel has been created by one of the best Patua scroll painters from Bengal, in collaboration with a fine writer and an innovative designer.

I See the Promised Land was conceived by Tara Books, a publisher with an ongoing interest in connecting Indian picture storytelling traditions with a contemporary reader's sensibility. One of Tara's most exciting dialogues has been with Patua artists – the Patua is a folk-art form that combines performance, storytelling and art. The story is recited or sung as the narrator holds up a painted scroll, pointing to the image that goes with the words.

The narrator tailors his rendering to suit the audience, and his repertoire ranges from traditional myths to current news stories. The Patua is a living tradition whose roots stretch back in time, but these talented artists and storytellers are our contemporaries. With energetic art and an intuitive grasp of narrative sequence, they are constantly looking for ways to take their work forward.

This was the basis of Tara's project: to nudge their work into exciting, more contemporary contexts. The process was a long and adventurous one, but it was apparent right away that the unfolding of the sequence of images in a Patua scroll – the manner in which the images are 'read,' one after the other – was more than halfway toward the structure of a modern graphic narrative. The art would have to be divided into panels, read sequentially from left to right rather than top to bottom, and the story would have to be written down, not just recited. To work at creating a graphic novel of a respectable length with a Patua artist involved a range of people and skills – from researcher to author to translator and designer.

That is another story. But Tara Books and Groundwood are delighted that the months of intensive –and pleasurable– work with the artists has now materialized from a vision of possibility to this exciting book.

Look for *Sita's Ramayana* by Samhita Arni and Moyna Chitrakar, another graphic novel inspired by the Patua scroll-art tradition.

ARTHUR FLOWERS TEACHES AT SYRACUSE UNIVERSITY IN THE ENGLISH DEPARTMENT'S MFA PROGRAM IN CREATIVE WRITING. A NATIVE OF MEMPHIS, HE HAS BEEN EXECUTIVE DIRECTOR OF THE HARLEM WRITERS GUILD, CO-FOUNDER OF THE NEW RENAISSANCE WRITERS GUILD AND THE PAN AFRICAN LITERARY FORUM. HE IS A BLUES-BASED PERFORMANCE POET WHO CONSIDERS HIMSELF LITERARY HEIR TO BOTH THE WESTERN WRITTEN TRADITION AND THE AFRICAN ORAL ONE. HE LIVES IN SYRACUSE, NEW YORK.

MANU CHITRAKAR LIVES AND WORKS IN NAYA VILLAGE IN BENGAL, INDIA. A PATUA SCROLL ARTIST WHO SINGS AND PAINTS, HE IS PART OF A LIVING ART AND PERFORMANCE TRADITION THAT IS AS OPEN TO CONTEMPORARY NEWS STORIES AND POLITICS, AS IT IS TO ANCIENT LEGEND AND MYTH.

GUGLIELMO ROSSI IS AN ITALIAN DESIGNER LIVING AND WORKING IN LONDON. HE STUDIED GRAPHIC DESIGN AT THE CENTRAL SAINT MARTINS COLLEGE OF ART AND DESIGN IN LONDON AND INDUSTRIAL DESIGN IN GENOA, ITALY.

I SEE THE PROMISED LAND, TEXT BY ARTHUR FLOWERS, ILLUSTRATIONS
BY MANU CHITRAKAR AND DESIGN BY GUGLIELMO ROSSI.

ORIGINAL EDITION COPYRIGHT © 2010 BY TARA BOOKS PVT. LTD., INDIA
(WWW.TARABOOKS.COM)
REVISED EDITION PUBLISHED IN CANADA AND THE USA IN 2013 BY
GROUNDWOOD BOOKS

GROUNDWOOD BOOKS / HOUSE OF ANANSI PRESS
110 SPADINA AVENUE, SUITE 801, TORONTO, ONTARIO M5V 2K4
OR C/O PUBLISHERS GROUP WEST
1700 FOURTH STREET, BERKELEY, CA 94710

WE ACKNOWLEDGE FOR THEIR FINANCIAL SUPPORT OF OUR PUBLISHING
PROGRAM THE GOVERNMENT OF CANADA THROUGH THE CANADA BOOK
FUND (CBF).

LIBRARY AND ARCHIVES CANADA CATALOGUING IN PUBLICATION
FLOWERS, A. R.
I SEE THE PROMISED LAND : A LIFE OF MARTIN LUTHER KING JR. / ARTHUR
FLOWERS ; [ILLUSTRATED BY] MANU CHITRAKAR. REV. ED.

ISBN 978-1-55498-328-5

1. KING, MARTIN LUTHER, JR., 1929-1968—JUVENILE LITERATURE. 2. AFRICAN
AMERICAN CIVIL RIGHTS WORKERS—BIOGRAPHY—JUVENILE LITERATURE.
3. AFRICAN AMERICANS—BIOGRAPHY—JUVENILE LITERATURE. 4. BAPTISTS—
UNITED STATES—CLERGY—BIOGRAPHY—JUVENILE LITERATURE. 5. AFRICAN
AMERICANS—CIVIL RIGHTS—HISTORY—20TH CENTURY—JUVENILE
LITERATURE. I. CHITRAKAR, MANU II. TITLE.

E185.97.K5F56 2013   J323.092   C2012-904190-4

THE ILLUSTRATIONS WERE MADE USING HOMEMADE NATURAL DYES ON PAPER.
PRODUCTION: C. ARUMUGAM
PRINTED AND BOUND IN CHINA